I0819425

21ST-CENTURY ECONOMICS

UNDERSTANDING THE STOCK MARKET

CHET'LA SEBREE

New York

Published in 2020 by Cavendish Square Publishing, LLC
243 5th Avenue, Suite 136, New York, NY 10016

First Edition

Library of Congress Cataloging-in-Publication Data

Names: Sebree, Chet'la, author.
Title: Understanding the stock market / Chet'la Sebree.
Description: First edition. | New York : Cavendish Square, 2020. |
Series: 21st-century economics | Includes bibliographical references and index.
Identifiers: LCCN 2018061307 (print) | LCCN 2019003473 (ebook) |
ISBN 9781502646071 (ebook) | ISBN 9781502646064 (library bound) |
ISBN 9781502646057 (pbk.)
Subjects: LCSH: Stock exchanges--Juvenile literature. | Investments--
Juvenile literature. | Finance--Juvenile literature.
Classification: LCC HG4553 (ebook) | LCC HG4553 .S43 2020 (print) |
DDC 332.64/2--dc23
LC record available at https://lccn.loc.gov/2018061307

Editorial Director: David McNamara
Copy Editor: Nathan Heidelberger
Associate Art Director: Alan Sliwinski
Designer: Joe Parenteau
Production Coordinator: Karol Szymczuk
Photo Research: J8 Media

Portions of this book originally appeared in *How the Stock Market Works* by Kathy Furgang.

The photographs in this book are used by permission and through the courtesy of: Cover, GotziLA Stock/Shutterstock.com; Abstract vector used throughout the book, Champ008/Shutterstock.com; p. 4 Lightspring/Shutterstock.com; p. 7 AshDesign/Shutterstock.com; pp. 8-9 Jitalia17/E+/Getty Images; p. 10 Moviestore collection Ltd/Alamy Stock Photo; p. 14 Bart Sadowski/Shutterstock.com; p. 15 Unknown/Private Collection/File: 1671newAmsterdam.jpg/Wikimedia Commons/Public Domain; pp. 17, 35 Bettmann/Getty Images; p. 21 Elias Goldensky (1868-1943)/File: FDR in 1933.jpg/Wikimedia Commons/Public Domain; p. 23 Henny Ray Abrams/AFP/Getty Images; p. 26 Schenectady Museum; Hall of Electrical History Foundation/Corbis/Getty Images; p. 30 Frederic Lewis/Getty Images; p. 32 American Stock/Archive Photos/Getty Images; p. 36 Library of Congress/Corbis/VCG/Getty Images; p. 38 Gabriele Giuseppini (https://www.panoramio.com/user/1413447?with_photo_id=14488280)/ https://www.panoramio.com/photo/14488280/File: Wall Street Bull, panoramio.jpg/Wikimedia Commons/CCA 3.0 Unported; p. 42 Sergiu Bacioiu (https://www.flickr.com/people/31191642@N05) from Romania/Water Drop, Explored (https://www.flickr.com/photos/sergiu_bacioiu/4178226353/)/File: Ripple effect on water.jpg/Wikimedia Commons/CCA-2.0 Generic; p. 45 Jim Watson/AFP/Getty Images; p. 49 Stephen Brashear/Getty Images; p. 50 AFP/Getty Images; p. 53 Nopparat Khokthong/Shutterstock.com; p. 56 Irina Mos/Shutterstock.com; p. 57 Oli Scarff/Getty Images; p. 62 Feifei Cui-Paoluzzo/Moment/Getty Images; p. 64 Casey Martin/Shutterstock.com; p. 66 Drew Angerer/Getty Images.

Printed in the United States of America

CONTENTS

INTRODUCTION

STOCKS, SHARES, AND BONDS

Ever heard a news anchor say the Dow Jones is up? Or one mention something about the NASDAQ? With these terms, you may also have heard an unfamiliar point system—the Dow is down 500 points. It's hard to turn on the television or look at a newspaper without seeing news about the stock market. Because of the unfamiliar terminology and point system, however, some people decide to completely ignore the reports about the stock market. These people often have not invested, or placed money into, the stock market. For that reason, they think that the market doesn't affect them. However, even if you don't have money in the stock market, the health of the market affects all of our everyday lives.

Opposite: People who invest in the stock market might enjoy periods of stability but should be prepared for the ups and downs the market regularly experiences.

Defining the Stock Market

The stock market, or stock exchange, is where buyers and sellers come together to facilitate the sale and purchase of shares, stocks, and bonds. A share is a unit of ownership in a company. Stocks are also units of ownership. Although these words are sometimes used interchangeably, "stock" is a more general term to discuss things bought and sold through the market. Meanwhile, "share" usually refers to specific certificates of ownership of a particular company. A bond is, essentially, a loan that an individual gives a company or government. The borrower agrees to pay back that loan with regular installments. Collectively, stocks, bonds, and shares are known as securities. A security is a certificate that proves a person's partial ownership of, or investment in, a company or government.

Although these terms surrounding the stock market may seem abstract, the market affects nearly everything we do. Primarily, it has a strong effect on our economy, which is the overall wealth of a region or country.

Why Invest?

One of the most important things that people should know is that the stock market is not a bank. When you put money in a bank, it is almost always safe. The bank will give the money back to a depositor whenever he or

A stock market ticker like this one or the one that runs through Times Square in New York City displays the changing prices of stocks along with other data about current market conditions.

she is ready to use it. That is not the case with the stock market. People who put their money in the stock market can lose it all if the stocks that they invest in go down, or lose value. They can also make more—sometimes

Although stocks, shares, and bonds can sound like abstract terms, it is important to remember that actual money backs these types of investments.

much more—than they invested if their stocks go up, or increase in value.

The stock market can be risky. So if the stock market is a risk, why do people invest in it? The potential to make

money prompts people to make investments despite the danger. It's this excitement and potential that has kept the stock market an important part of the United States' economy for more than a century.

CHAPTER 1

THE BASICS

You've probably seen a movie that featured a scene with a stock market. For instance, the fictional Gotham Stock Exchange is featured in the Batman movie *The Dark Knight Rises*. The villain Bane holds up the Gotham Stock Exchange in order to make a poor investment for Bruce Wayne (Batman). He wants Wayne to lose all of the money he's invested in the stock market. In the scene, there are hundreds of traders on the floor. In real life, in places like the New York Stock Exchange (NYSE), these traders rush across a crowded floor, chatter on phones, and yell back and forth to each other as they wave little pieces of paper in the air. All the while, they glance up at numbers that flash on computer screens and electronic scrolls that

Opposite: In *The Dark Knight Rises*, Bane (*right*) makes a bad investment for Bruce Wayne, and Wayne loses all of his money. Although this is just a movie, people do lose money in the market.

surround them. They are helping people all around the world buy and sell stocks.

What's What and Who's Who

A stock market is a place that sells shares. When someone owns one or more shares of a company, he or she is known as a shareholder. This person becomes part owner of that company. Anyone who puts his or her money into the stock market by buying shares of companies is called an investor. An investor hopes to make a profit with his or her investment. There are many opportunities to make money in the stock market. If a company does well, its profits go up, and shareholders make money. However, if a company does not do well and its profits slow or decrease, a shareholder may lose money.

The people who run around the stock exchange floor are called stockbrokers. They work all day to help people buy or sell shares of companies. Suppose a company is selling its shares for $10 each. An investor might want to buy ten shares. He or she pays $100 and then owns a very small portion of the company. The investor may make more money than he or she spent on the stock purchase if the company does well and makes a profit. A company that sells shares of its company to the public is called a public company. Companies "go public" and sell stock in order to raise more money to operate. They use this money to hire more employees, to expand operations, and to research and develop new products. As a company makes more of a profit, the price of its shares increases. Shareholders can hold on to these shares or sell them for a profit.

Additionally, when a company makes profits, it can distribute some of these profits to shareholders. The money a company gives its shareholders on a regular basis based on its profits is called a dividend. Dividends are usually given out each quarter year. A small amount, usually less than a dollar, is given for each share that a stockholder owns. For example, if a shareholder owns one thousand shares of a company and the company offers a forty-cent dividend for each share, the stockholder will receive $400 each quarter. This is another way shareholders can make money in the stock market.

The History of Wall Street

The financial center of the US economy is located at the southern tip of Manhattan on a narrow street called Wall Street. This is the site of the New York Stock Exchange. This building is where most stock buying and selling is done in the United States. This constant buying and selling of stocks is known as trading.

The history of Wall Street goes back almost four hundred years, long before there was even a nation known as the United States. Dutch explorers and colonists

In the twenty-first century, most trading at the New York Stock Exchange, pictured here, is conducted on computers, tablets, and smartphones.

settled Manhattan back in 1626. At this time, they named the settlement New Amsterdam. It was part of New Netherland, a Dutch colony stretching from Cape Cod in the north to the Delmarva Peninsula in the south. In 1653, the Dutch built a 12-foot (3.7-meter) wall in Lower Manhattan that spanned from the East River to the Hudson

New Amsterdam, which would become New York after it was seized by the British, was originally settled by the Dutch in the seventeenth century.

River. The Dutch hoped the wall would protect them from the Native Americans and British. After the wall was torn down in the late seventeenth century, Wall Street was built where the defensive wall originally stood.

From the beginning, Wall Street was a central meeting place for merchants who wished to trade commodities. Commodities are goods that have not been processed yet, such as raw wheat, tobacco, or cotton. Even enslaved laborers who had been forcibly brought from countries in Africa were traded on Wall Street, which was near one of the city's main ports.

In the mid-1700s, about a century after Britain seized control of Manhattan and the entire New Netherland colony from the Dutch, the thirteen colonies began to experience issues with Great Britain. Rebellions began to break out. Lower Manhattan was a common place for protest. In fact, during the American Revolution (1776–1783), many houses along Wall Street were burned down. They were most likely burned by colonists who didn't want to surrender the city to the British.

The Founding of the New York Stock Exchange

In May 1792, following the revolution, a group of twenty-four brokers decided to form a group devoted to the selling of public stocks. They would be paid by other

The first stock exchange in New York was formed by the signing of the Buttonwood Agreement under a tree at 68 Wall Street in May 1792.

people to trade stocks for them. The brokers signed an agreement under a buttonwood tree at 68 Wall Street. They continued to do their work there for years, moving to a coffeehouse in the winter. The document they signed is known as the Buttonwood Agreement. It formed the first formal New York stock exchange. In March 1817, the organization created a constitution and was officially renamed the New York Stock and Exchange Board. The same year, they moved operations to a rented room at 40 Wall Street.

Brokers had to belong to the New York Stock Exchange in order to do business there. That did not stop outside brokers from earning money on their own, however. These outside brokers traded securities right on the street corners of Wall Street.

Capitalism and the Stock Market

Can the public be part owners of companies around the world? Do all countries sell and trade shares in their public companies? Most of them do, but not all. The system that allows the United States and many other countries to trade and sell goods and shares of companies is called capitalism.

According to the ideas of capitalism, people develop and sell goods or services for a profit. The stocks of companies that provide products or services that are in high demand usually rise. More people are interested in these companies because they are developing popular products or services, selling a lot of units, and making a lot of money. The rise in stock prices is good for shareholders because, if they sell their shares, they can get more money for each one. Similarly, the rise in stock prices signals a potential rise in their quarterly dividends.

Companies that do not have successful products may find that their stock prices are dropping. People are not willing to take a risk and invest in that company if they don't feel its profits are rising and its products are good or desirable. The supply and demand of a company's stock often corresponds to the success of the goods or services the company offers. If demand for a company's products is high, its stock tends to be in high demand too, so the stock price rises. The opposite is true for a company whose products and services are not in high demand among consumers.

In twenty-first-century markets, people buy and sell goods that are made by companies worldwide. This international buying and selling of goods and services leads to the international buying and selling of stock. For instance, foreign investors can buy stock in American companies, and vice versa. There are more than fifty major stock exchanges worldwide that handle this sort of trading on the global market.

US SECURITIES AND EXCHANGE COMMISSION

The US Securities and Exchange Commission (SEC) was created by the Securities Exchange Act of 1934. It was created in response to the stock market crash of 1929, one of the sharpest declines in stock values in history. For many, the crash marked the beginning of the Great Depression. This was a period in which people struggled to provide their families with basic necessities like food and shelter.

The SEC was created as a part of the New Deal programs, which were geared toward helping the economy recover from the Great Depression. The first chairman of the SEC was Joseph P. Kennedy, the father of future president John F. Kennedy. He was appointed to the position by President Franklin Delano Roosevelt.

According to the SEC's website, its mission "is to protect investors; maintain fair, orderly, and efficient markets; and facilitate capital formation." In other words, the commission is responsible for making sure that the buying and selling of stocks, the operation of the stock market, and the accumulation of wealth happen in legal ways. For instance, it oversees the work of stockbrokers. The SEC makes sure that stockbrokers appropriately carry out the wishes of their clients. In the twenty-first century, the SEC also regulates exchanges that occur between companies worldwide as the United States trades with international businesses as well.

President Franklin Delano Roosevelt created programs to help lift the country out of the Great Depression. The Securities and Exchange Commission is one that still exists today.

The Importance of Stock Indexes

Although it is not the only stock exchange, the NYSE is the largest in the world in terms of market value. Market value is the amount for which something can be sold on the open market. Each year, trillions of dollars of stock are traded through the NYSE on four trading room floors. At the NYSE, brokers do the buying and selling at the direction of their customers, who place orders.

The National Association of Securities Dealers Automated Quotations (NASDAQ) is also another major stock exchange based in New York. The NASDAQ, founded in 1971, is important for both brokers and investors. It is an electronic stock exchange, where brokers can buy and sell stocks via computer. Several thousand companies trade their securities through this exchange. It has more trading volume per hour than any other exchange in the world.

There are several ways an investor can keep track of how the stock market is performing. One way to track performance of stocks is through stock indexes. A stock index is a measurement of the performance of the stock of a sample collection of companies. There are three popular indexes in the United States that people use to review stock results. They are the NASDAQ Composite, the Dow Jones Industrial Average (often referred to as

In addition to general tickers, there are different monitors for indexes that displays graphs, information about market volumes, and track changes over the days and weeks.

"the Dow Jones" or "the Dow"), and the Standard and Poor's 500 (the S&P 500). To clarify, the NASDAQ is an index as well as a stock exchange. When the news reports that "the NASDAQ gained 100 points today," that means the collective value of the stocks chosen for the NASDAQ index went up by that number of points.

When the point value of the NASDAQ is reported, a percentage gain or loss is also reported. This is a more important indicator of how the stock market did that day. It may have gained 2 percent or lost 1.5 percent of its cumulative value. The cumulative value represents the total worth of the stock of the companies in the index. These numbers let investors know if the stock market as a whole is gaining or losing value, since the companies in the index are supposed to represent the larger economy.

Business news reports also often state that "the Dow was up today" or "the Dow Jones took a hit today." The Dow Jones Industrial Average is another kind of index that gives an overall sense of how the stock market is doing. There is no way to quickly report the results of every company during the day, so the Dow is an average of the thirty most widely held and largest companies in the United States. The Dow does not indicate how every company that is publicly traded performed. It is simply an average of some of the biggest of them.

Similarly, the S&P 500 is another index for reporting stock averages. It is an index of five hundred companies. The companies with larger holdings carry a greater weight on the index than the smaller ones.

The Stock Market and the Economy

Together, all of these figures help people determine the health of not just the stocks but the overall economy. If the economy is doing well, people are usually investing in businesses because they have the money to invest. Similarly, the economy does well if the businesses continue to make good profits, which encourages more people to invest.

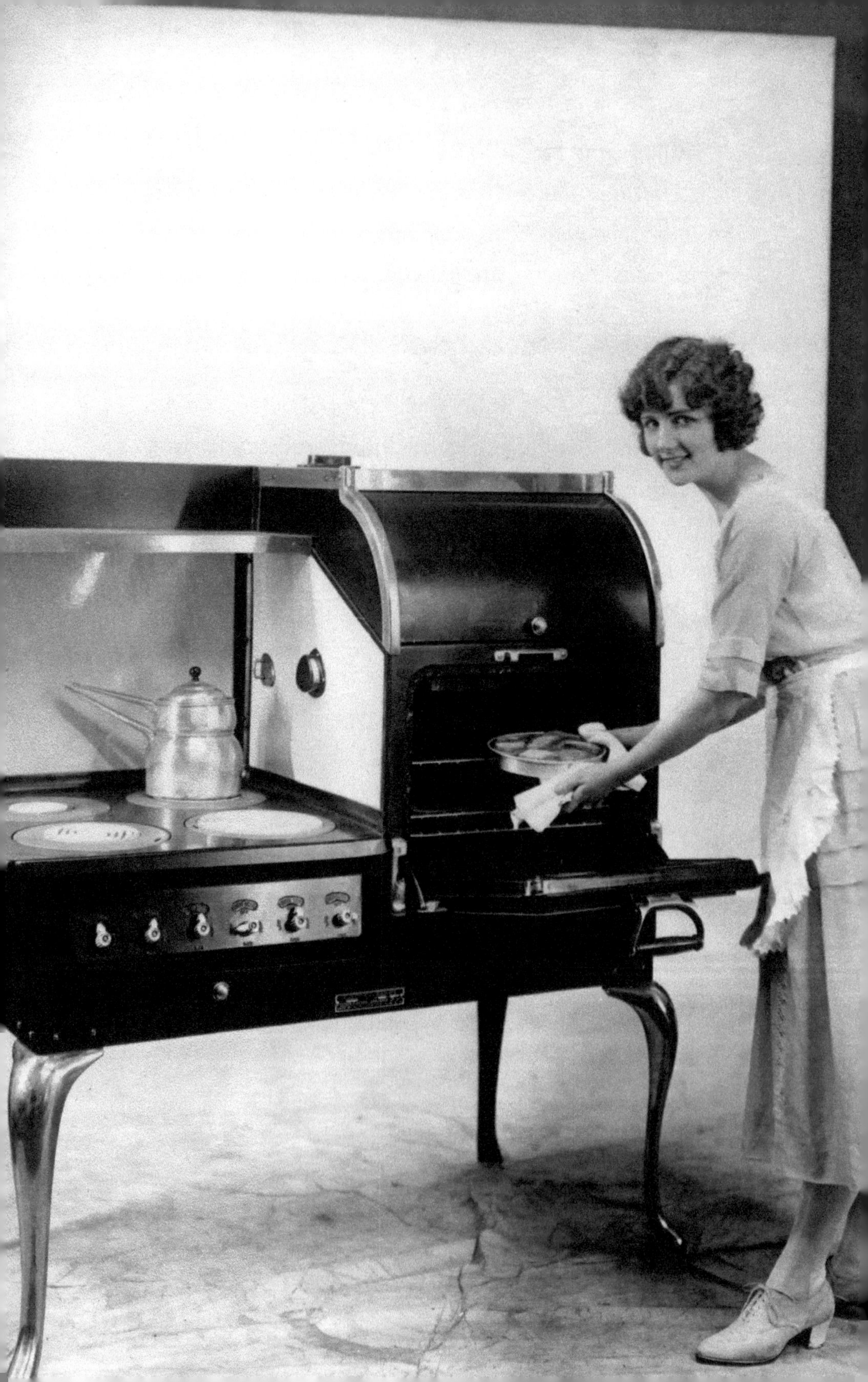

CHAPTER 2

ITS EFFECT ON DAILY LIFE

You might wonder how the stock market affects your everyday life or that of those around you. For those who are not investors or who do not work for a publicly traded company, the connection may be difficult to see. However, a good example of how the stock market ultimately affects everyone is provided by the Great Depression in the United States during the 1930s.

The Roaring Twenties

To fully understand the Great Depression, it helps to look at the years that came before the biggest economic downturn in US history. The 1920s were a time of great prosperity in the United States. World War I was over. There were many new inventions and technologies offering an

Opposite: As new technologies were created and people enjoyed relative financial comfort in the 1920s, stock prices for companies like General Electric and Westinghouse soared.

easier life for people at home, including refrigerators, telephones, and radios.

It was a time when many large companies rose and became popular with the public. Companies like General Electric and Westinghouse proved that they could make a lot of money for their investors. They inspired such confidence that more ordinary people invested their money in these corporations. For the first time, investing in the stock market became more commonplace for the average American. People who did not even have the cash to buy stocks could borrow money from the bank, invest, wait for their stock prices to rise, and then use some of their profits to pay back the bank loan.

The era became known as the Roaring Twenties. This was an unusual economic time. Stock prices kept rising because more and more people were investing in companies. Many newer and first-time investors did not know much about the companies they were investing in. They merely made guesses about the companies based on their names or what they thought the company produced. Everyone expected to make a profit overnight. Some stocks rose from $20 to $300 a share in just a matter of months.

The Stock Market Crash of 1929

As the 1920s came to an end, so did the "roaring" and prosperous days of the stock market. In September 1929, stock prices began to slip. But just as soon as they fell, the prices seemed to recover. As October came, dips in the market became more common. The market seemed less of a sure thing. Investors were more nervous about the economy and less willing to pour money into stocks. People were no longer confident that their stocks were going to be a way to keep making money. As people sold off their stocks and stopped investing in new ones, stock prices slipped further.

On Wednesday, October 23, a sudden and large rush of investors wanted to sell their stocks, all in the last hour of trading. It was a shock to the market. Some stock prices dropped more than $10 in that final hour, an equivalent of almost $150 in 2018. More than 2.5 million shares were traded during that short time. As the closing bell rang, investors were panicked. The stock market was beginning to crash.

The next day, Thursday, October 24, the panic continued. A huge stock market crash was underway, driven largely by people's fears. Fear and panic can cause investors to pull their money out of an investment quickly and cause prices to plummet. As the NYSE opened Thursday morning, investors began selling immediately. There seemed to be no one willing to buy up these shares. By the end of the day, the total value of dumped stocks was $14 billion. That would have been over $200 billion in 2018.

BY 10 O'CLOCK TONIGHT

BER 25, 1929 WEATHER—Cloudy abcdefg TWO CENTS

STOCK VALUES CRASH IN RECORD STAMPEDE; BANKERS HALT ROUT

CURIOUS JAM WALL STREET TO SEE THE 'SHOW'

Huge Crowd Throngs "Money Lane" Seeking Thrill in Battle of Bulls and Bears

Butcher, Baker and Candlestick Maker Rush to View "World Series" of Finance

From The Inquirer Bureau.
NEW YORK, Oct. 24.—Huge crowds in a holiday mood resembling a confetti of faces from the upper stories of Wall Street skyscrapers surged up and down the narrow

Stock Slump Fails to Dim Tax Cut Hope

WASHINGTON, Oct. 24 (A. P.).—The view that the recent slumps in the stock market will not affect the administration's tax-reduction programme is held by Treasury officials.

The officials regard the slumps as being more in paper profits than in actual values and believe the action was in the nature of a readjustment of the market and that stock prices generally still were above those paid by people who bought them at ordinary stages some time ago.

BUSINESS OF NATION UNSHAKEN, DECLARE TREASURY OFFICIALS

Officials Assert Under-

UPSWING ENDS WILD SELLING IN 12,894,650 DAY

N. Y. Exchange Sees Most Violent Drop in Prices Since 1914; Ticker Hours Late

Market Rallies as Morgan and Other Financial Groups Meet and Issue Statement Declaring Trade Sound

From The Inquirer Bureau.
NEW YORK, Oct. 24.—Long withheld buying powers and the reassuring statements of America's most powerful banking interests came to the support of a collapsing stock market today and

bout the doors of
es in Wall Street

STUDENT,
INCE JUNE,

On Friday, October 25, 1929, newspapers were filled with articles about Black Thursday and the massive sale of stocks.

In 1929, the figure was unbelievably large. The entire annual budget of the US government at the time was only $3 billion. Nearly five times the annual budget of the country was lost in just one day of trading.

The panic on Wall Street did not stop there. Over the next few days of trading, more and more investors sold off their stocks for increasingly low prices. Black Tuesday,

October 29, was the darkest day on Wall Street. More than $8 billion more in stock values disappeared. From Wednesday, October 23 to Tuesday, October 29, the stock market lost more than $25 billion.

As word spread of the stock market crash and people had less hope for its quick recovery, insecurity about money spread from the stock market to the banking industry. Banks had lent out a lot of money to stock market investors. The hope was that the investor could make money in stocks and then pay back the bank with interest. Interest is the amount a bank charges a person for borrowing money.

After the stock market collapsed, many banks were left with no money on hand. Most of it was loaned out, and there was no chance the borrowers would be able to repay it. Depositors rushed to their banks to withdraw their money, fearing that the banks would fail due to these bad loans. The banks did not have enough to hand out to everyone who wished to withdraw their money. Today, there are laws to prevent this from happening. However, back then, people lost their entire life savings. In this way, not everyone who lost everything was a stock market investor.

Crash Contributes to Decade-Long Depression

After people lost their money due to plummeting stock prices or bank failures, many had to sell their possessions in order to raise enough money for basic necessities like clothes, food, and shelter. People sold their cars, houses, and jewelry. Given the widespread economic collapse and suffering, though, people usually received rock-bottom prices for these valuables. And these struggles, unfortunately, were just the beginning.

The full effects of the stock market crash would not be felt for months and even years. Companies that saw their stocks plummet had little money left to operate, produce goods, or pay employees. Unemployment rose

Although economists generally agree the stock market crash alone did not cause the Great Depression, it certainly marked the beginning of devastating financial times.

as companies went through difficult times and laid off workers. By 1933, one out of every four white Americans was out of work. Nearly 50 percent of African Americans could not find work. People could not pay their mortgages, which are loans for homes or land. Failure to pay these loans resulted in these people losing their homes and farms. Families suffering from unemployment could not spend on consumer goods or entertainment. This caused other businesses, such as restaurants and stores, to go out of business. As a result, even more workers were laid off. Once-wealthy businessmen were forced to sell whatever they could on street corners in order to make enough money to eat. People set up wooden or cardboard shelters in city parks to live in. Millions of people who had never invested a dime in the stock market were impoverished, hungry, unemployed, and desperate.

Recovery

The entire decade of the 1930s was difficult for Americans. President Franklin Roosevelt tried to fix the economy with a massive economic stimulus plan called the New Deal. These sorts of stimulus plans are geared toward renewing economic growth.

The New Deal put people back to work building bridges, roads, schools, libraries, public office buildings, and other important and useful structures. This provided the families of these workers with money for life's basic necessities, like food, clothing, and shelter. Additionally, the New Deal programs helped improve the nation's transportation infrastructure at a time when more good, paved roads and safe, convenient bridges were needed.

An important part of Roosevelt's response to the Great Depression was the creation of the Securities and Exchange Commission (SEC). The SEC protects investors by monitoring and regulating the sale of stocks in the stock market. It oversees the work of stockbrokers to make sure that they are carrying out the wishes of their clients. The Federal Deposit Insurance Corporation, or FDIC, was another Roosevelt creation. It also protects the American people from losing money. The FDIC insures the money that people deposit into their checking and savings accounts. This means that the government guarantees that it will cover the amount of money owed to depositors if the bank does not have the money to do so.

Despite all of this government intervention, the Great Depression didn't really end until the United States joined the World War II war effort. At this time, thousands of Americans were needed to make goods for the war, such as tanks, planes, jeeps, battleships, artillery, armor, ammunition, and uniforms. Factories opened and wartime materials were produced in large quantities. Workers—mainly women, since the young men were off fighting the

World War II war production helped pull the country out of the Great Depression. It also offered many women the opportunity to join the workforce for the first time.

war—were put to work in factories and even on the stock market trading floor. Stocks in companies that produced goods for the war effort became stable and strong again.

By the time the war ended, the country had recovered from the Great Depression. People were able to afford not only basic necessities but luxury items. By the 1950s, many people purchased new homes and appliances for these new homes to make life simpler. In fact, in 1950, the United States was the richest country in the world.

THE INVENTION OF THE TICKER TAPE

Stockbrokers must be able to communicate prices to each other in order to buy and sell stocks. In the early 1800s, messengers raced back and forth between brokerage houses with hand-written orders to buy and sell stocks.

Infamous stockbroker Thomas William Lawson waits as ticker tape data rolls in. Lawson was known for suspicious stock manipulations.

Sharing information with stock exchanges in other cities was more difficult. Men used flags to signal the prices of stocks. People set up along an intercity route used telescopes to read, record, and pass on this information to the next person along the route.

Both of these methods were replaced with Morse code after Samuel Morse invented the telegraph in 1844. Morse code is a telecommunication system. It uses established sequences of signal durations. These signal durations, called dots and dashes, correspond to a standardized list of text characters. In this way, the code can transmit messages from one place to another.

By 1867, the ticker tape machine was invented. This allowed all of the brokerage houses to get the same information at the same time along a long strip of paper called a ticker tape. The information on the ticker tape was in Morse code. A clerk would receive the message and then write the stock prices on a board for everyone to see. Eventually, this method was replaced with electronic displays.

In the twenty-first century, stock prices instantly flash on television, computer, and cell phone screens around the world. There are even huge scrolling electronic tickers in public places, like New York City's Times Square.

NO PARKING
TUNNEL
TRUCK ROUTE
LOCAL

CHAPTER 3

HIGHS AND LOWS

Experienced investors know that the stock market will always go through periods of expansion and contraction. The term used to describe a period of faster growth and prosperity is "bull market." Like a bull, the market charges on, strong and fierce. During a bull market, stock prices rise, and investors make a lot of money. A period of economic slowdown is called a bear market. Some believe the term "bear market" has its roots in the old proverb "to sell the bear's skin before one has caught the bear." The phrase means to sell something you don't yet have. The market normally moves slowly between bull and bear markets.

Opposite: The bull sculpture on Wall Street is meant to symbolize a bull market—a prosperous financial market.

Economic Highs and Lows

Similar to the stock market, the economy goes through natural highs and lows. It's all a part of the business cycle, which has periods of expansion and contraction. A period of good economic growth is known as a period of expansion. During these periods, it seems almost effortless for investors to make money. Companies hire a lot of workers. Salaries and job security are good. Money is flowing, and consumer confidence is high as a result. The public spends money on not only things they need but things they want. However, economic upswings don't last forever. It is natural for the economy to slow down. A period in which the economy slows down is called a recession. During a recession, companies produce fewer goods, they need fewer employees, and people spend less money. A recession can be a very trying period for all members of a society.

The Effect of Recessions

Like throwing a stone into a pond, a problem in one area of the economy can have a ripple effect causing issues in other parts of an economy, leading to a recession. When companies need fewer workers, they must lay people off in order to continue to make a profit. At the same time, they are making fewer goods because consumer demand has gone down. Laid-off workers will have less money to spend in their everyday lives because they no longer get a regular paycheck. They will not be able to buy new goods such as cars, televisions, clothing, and furniture. They will have less money to go to the movies, restaurants, and amusement parks.

The more companies that lay off people during a recession, the more people there are who cannot keep the economy running through consumer spending. Eventually, people who have been laid off may not be able to pay their rent or their mortgages. Even those workers who hang on to their jobs may be worried about being laid off in the near future. For that reason, they cut back on their household spending and begin to save money instead.

When fewer people spend money, however, the economy slows even more. The companies that let go of workers now sell even fewer goods than before. So they make even smaller profits (or no profits at all) and may have to lay off even more workers. As a result, the companies' stock prices will fall. This fall in stock prices reflects the fact that consumers aren't purchasing their goods and that they aren't making good profits.

As a result, investors in these companies are no longer making any money. They may begin to lose confidence in the companies they have invested their money in. Investors may sell their stock, and those companies then have even less money to help them get through the difficult

Elements of the economy are interconnected. A slowdown in one business sector, such as the automotive industry, can have a ripple effect on other sectors and lead to a recession.

times. Some companies can no longer make a profit and may fail altogether, declaring bankruptcy and going out of business.

The more businesses that slow down, the more people are affected throughout the economy at all income levels. It can take months or even years, but the ripple effects of a recession can reach specific regions of the country, the nation at large, and even the world markets.

Recessions and Bubble Bursts

Many things can bring about a recession. However, often it's the period of expansion itself that indirectly causes an eventual slowdown. All of the companies that are involved in making the goods and services sold to consumers will be doing great. If the companies are public, their stocks will likely be soaring. Their investors will be happy that they are making money. The companies themselves will probably need to hire extra workers to keep up with the extra production needed to meet the increased demand for products and services. Hiring and salaries will probably increase. During a time when people have extra money to spend, they may decide to make "big ticket," or major, purchases, like a new car or a vacation home.

But how many extra cars and homes can people buy? How long can companies' stocks soar as people buy these new products? The unusually high demand for a particular good or service is often called a bubble. But what happens to bubbles after a while? They burst. Like any other bubble, goods and services bubbles eventually burst. This means there suddenly won't be a great demand for the products that people bought in good economic times. The companies will need to produce fewer of these products. As a result, they will not be able to employ as many workers.

Unemployed workers or employees who fear unemployment will drastically cut their spending, resulting in still lower levels of product production, more layoffs, and even less consumer spending. This will cause a downward spiral throughout the economy that keeps worsening as time goes on. As these industries suffer, so do their stock prices.

Recession Management

How do recessions end? Money has to be injected back into the economy through investments, public spending, and greater access to loans and credit. Presidents who lead during economic slowdowns often try to do something to help the economy get back on its feet and start producing again. In an attempt to end the Great Depression, President Franklin Delano Roosevelt introduced the New Deal in the 1930s. The New Deal gave money to people who needed loans. It also introduced massive public spending and construction projects, such as the building of roads, bridges, and government buildings. The projects put many people back to work and eventually brought money back into the economy.

Another way to inject cash back into a stalled economy and stimulate upward movement in the stock market is for the government to give its citizens money to spend as they wish. In 2008, while George W. Bush was president,

President Barack Obama (*left*) and President George W. Bush (*right*) used different tactics to try to help the economy recover from the Great Recession.

the US economy entered a major economic downturn called the Great Recession. To stimulate the economy, the Bush administration sent tax rebate checks to US citizens that they could spend in any way they saw fit. The hope was that they would use the money to buy goods or services, putting money back into a weak economy. This, however, did not keep the US economy from sliding into a recession.

When Barack Obama became president in 2009, the government took a different approach to fighting the recession. His administration gave money to various private organizations and state governments. For instance, major lending and insurance companies like Freddie Mac and American International Group (AIG) were struggling financially. Similarly, major companies in the automotive industry like General Motors were having financial difficulties. The infusion of money to some of these organizations and companies was done in order to save businesses, create more jobs, and prevent the country from sliding into an even deeper recession.

In fact, President Obama's stimulus plan functioned similarly to the New Deal. It focused on providing jobs that might help improve the nation's roads, bridges, and buildings. It also focused on increasing green technologies. These are technologies that would help reduce the country's dependence on nonrenewable and environmentally harmful resources, such as fossil fuels. The hope was that the stimulated economy would inspire people to invest in stocks again.

QUICK Q&A

Did anyone see the stock market crash of 1929 coming?

Yes. There were a few people who predicted that stock prices could not continue to stay as high as they were. Some investors observed the dwindling money supply in banks, the huge amount of cash lent out to investors, and the highly inflated prices of stocks. They knew that a problem was bound to arise. They correctly saw that a slump in stock prices would result in widespread defaults on these loans and a cash crisis for the banks, which would not be able to cover the deposits of their ordinary customers.

Did the stock market crash cause the Great Depression?

No. Many economists believe that the country was already entering a recession at the time the stock market crashed. The period of prosperity had allowed many Americans to buy goods such as cars, homes, telephones, and radios. However, the demand for the products had begun to decrease during the late 1920s. Unemployment had already been rising before the stock market crash. It actually may have been the weakening economy that prompted the crash.

What should someone consider before investing in the stock market?

You want to be reasonably sure that your stock will do well. So you must consider what the company you want to invest in does, the state of the industry the company is in, and the current economic times. For example, when the radio was first invented, investors bought shares of companies that manufactured radios, supplied radio parts, and produced and broadcast radio programs. Then, times changed. Entertainment technology evolved. When television came along, there were fewer investors in radio. Investment dollars began to flow to television and its related fields. The trick is to invest in smaller companies about to release an innovative breakthrough product or patent a revolutionary technology that will become the "next big thing." Once this new product or technology hits the market and generates buzz, excitement, and demand, the company's stock price will rise quickly.

People who invested in Amazon early now have made a lot of money. In addition to being one of the biggest online retailers, the company develops new technologies like the Echo Dot, shown here.

Paw Prints
Paw Prints
King Queen
King Queen

CHAPTER 4

THE TWENTY-FIRST-CENTURY MARKET

There have been several events in the twenty-first century that have affected the stock market, such as the dot-com bubble and housing bubble bursts. Both of these events caused economic downturns that affected investors.

Dot-Com Bubble Burst

In the late twentieth century, the internet was still a new, mostly unexplored world. Suddenly everyone was talking about cyberspace, the World Wide Web, and the information superhighway. There was also a lot of money to be made in this new cyberworld.

Start-up companies sprang up everywhere to meet this new and sudden demand for content on the internet. Even

Opposite: International relationships affect the stock market. In 2018, the US-Chinese trade war affected the US purchase of Chinese goods, which affected both countries' markets.

though the information technology (IT) industry was just getting started, investors eagerly snatched up the stock of IT start-up companies. They did so even when these companies had yet to produce and market an actual product or service.

Web companies with web addresses that ended in ".com" (short for "commerce") became the recipients of millions of dollars of investors' money. Some of these companies offered little more than a ".com" in their name. They often had no plan, no product, and no income other than investors' money.

Nevertheless, these companies felt confident that they had something to offer the public. Investors gave them millions of dollars for their initial public offering, or IPO. That means investors gave a company enough money to issue stock to the public at a certain price. A dot-com bubble occurred because people invested an incredible amount of money, often in companies that had nothing to offer or sell. Stock prices were far higher than the actual companies, their products, and their potential were worth.

Just because a company has a good idea doesn't mean that the idea will succeed. Plenty of entrepreneurs put their ideas to work during the dot-com bubble of the late 1990s. When their dreams did not come true, thousands of workers were laid off. Wall Street suffered from plummeting stock prices. By 2001, many of these

Although many companies failed during the dot-com bubble burst, a few, like Google, Amazon, and eBay, survived.

companies failed and went out of business. Their investors lost thousands, and sometimes millions, of dollars. The country sank into a recession, affecting people who did not work or invest in the IT industry.

Not every dot-com went under, however. Some of the companies we now use regularly and rely upon got their starts during the era of the dot-com bubble. Google, Amazon, and eBay are all dot-com success stories.

The Housing Bubble

While this dot-com bubble was building and bursting, another industry experienced a boom. During the late

1990s and first half of the 2000s, there was a financial boom in the real estate industry. It became easier for people to get a mortgage. Normally, a mortgage is based on the income of the potential buyer as well as the person's credit history. A credit history is based on a person's track record of previously paying bills and repaying loans. However, in the early 2000s, banks were more relaxed and lent money to people who could not actually afford the houses they bought. They didn't have enough income, and often they had poor credit histories.

Mortgages given to people with poor credit histories are called subprime mortgages. Usually, banks are hesitant to issue them because there is a risk the borrower won't be able to pay back the loan. However, during this period, banks freely approved subprime mortgages in hopes of making extra money from these high-risk borrowers. For example, these mortgages often came with interest rates that started low but rose over time. New homeowners' payments could go up dramatically and sometimes unexpectedly after just a few months. This often put the monthly mortgage payments beyond the range of what the new homeowners could afford.

Predatory lending practices such as this were ignored by bank regulating authorities, mainly because home prices kept rising along with demand. This meant that banks kept making more and more profits. They weren't the only ones.

Construction workers enjoyed the boom in new home building. The stock market enjoyed the rising profits and stock prices of banks, mortgage lenders, and other financial institutions. All of this lending, spending, building, and buying occurred in part because the government's central bank, the Federal Reserve, was being especially hands-off. It was not carefully monitoring or regulating the business practices of many lenders and other financial institutions.

The Great Recession

Buyers in over their heads, reckless lenders, and inattentive federal government practices all played a role in creating the housing bubble and the economic crisis that followed its bursting. People who could not truly afford their subprime mortgages began defaulting on their loans, meaning they failed to make the payments. This caused banks to foreclose on people's homes. This meant the people had to move out of their homes, which would be seized and sold off by the banks that had issued their mortgages. Since the banks owned the homes, they kept any money raised by their sale. This, however, would not fix the crisis banks faced.

When the housing bubble burst, many construction projects were abandoned. Additionally, people who had purchased homes lost their houses because they were unable to pay back loans.

Banks had made so many reckless loans that would not be repaid that they could no longer cover all the deposits made by their customers with checking and savings accounts. Banks began to fail, and mortgage companies entered a crisis. In some cases, the government had to step in and use money from the Federal Reserve to cover bank losses. Billions of dollars were lost by these banks and mortgage companies even before the stock market crashed.

In early 2008, major financial institutions and mortgage lenders started facing the grim reality. Many of these institutions had mortgage-backed securities. These types of securities are debt securities. Debt securities are certificates that represent borrowed money that will eventually need to be repaid. These companies were hoping to repay these debt securities with the money they'd make from subprime mortgages. As people began to default on their mortgages, however, these institutions were no longer able to repay their loans either. As banks failed to pay back their loans, they either sold to other banks, received an influx of money from the government, or failed entirely.

The failure of major financial institutions frightened their investors, who started selling off stock and moving

Lehman Brothers, a major investment bank, collapsed in the wake of the Great Recession.

their money to safer industries and corporations. On September 29, 2008, the stock market crashed. Between October 2008 and March 2009, markets continued to free-fall. At the same time that stocks were suffering, more and more people lost their homes. Bank failures left banks unable to lend money to average citizens and companies that needed loans. Consumers stopped spending. Companies were forced to lay off workers. Less money went into the economy. The cycle of economic decline sped up quickly.

By 2009, most Americans were affected in some manner. Problems now existed in sectors other than the mortgage and banking industries. For instance, in late 2008, the automotive industry found itself in trouble. Two major companies, General Motors and Chrysler, found themselves near bankruptcy. If these businesses had gone under, it would have cost nearly a million people their jobs. Unemployment was already up to nearly 10 percent around the country. Although this economic downturn was not as severe as that of the 1930s, the financial crisis was intense.

With a weak economy comes hard times. Small businesses failed because they could not get loans from banks to continue their operations. Larger companies and state and federal governments were forced to cut their budgets to make up for lost revenue. Companies

RESPONSE TO CRISIS

Just as the United States in 2008 slid into a financial crisis, Americans were choosing a new commander in chief. The new president, Barack Obama, was faced with the tough decision of how to fix the economy. Should the federal government stay out of economic policy, as some economists suggested, and let market forces correct the problems? Or should the government attempt to reverse the economic free-fall and protect its citizens from the harshest effects of the recession?

In his 2008 campaign, Barack Obama expressed a strong commitment to being active and aggressive in his attempts to revive the economy. In early 2009, the House of Representatives approved an economic recovery plan of over $700 billion. It would take time for the money to be fully distributed and for consumers and investors to regain confidence in the economy. By July 2009, however, markets finally started to recover. The stock market collapse was over.

closing their doors or reducing production meant falling stock prices. Meanwhile, a lack of consumer confidence left investors hesitant to invest, which further affected the stock market.

Additionally, the financial difficulties of the United States also affected the rest of the world. The United States does so much business with companies around the globe that it was hard for other economies and stock markets not to be affected. Cutbacks in production and reduced overseas demand for US products translated into fewer exports. The collapse in American consumer spending translated into fewer imports. As a result, both American and international companies experienced a sales slump and had to lay off workers. Economies around the world suffered. So did the stock prices of US and foreign companies. The recession that began with the burst bubble in the American housing industry went global.

Another Crisis

These two bubble bursts have not been the only issues to affect the stock market in the twenty-first century. The stock market is affected just as much by political relationships as it is by industries.

In December 2018, economists noted that the stock market in the United States had experienced its worst

December since the Great Depression. Economists found these struggles in the stock market unusual because the economy was strong and the unemployment rate was low in the United States at the time. Usually, a strong economy and low unemployment rate correspond to a bull market.

Many economists thought that the downturn in the stock market stemmed from issues between China and the United States. At the time, the two countries were in the midst of an argument about tariffs, or the taxes placed on goods imported and exported between countries. Investors, fearful of how high tariffs could affect the demand on foreign-produced goods in either country, watched the markets carefully. Some economists predicted that there would be a recession in 2019 because of both the tariff disagreements and the hesitant investors.

Investment Realities

The stock market is not always a roller-coaster ride, characterized by dramatic peaks and stomach-churning drops. The general trend of the stock market in the United States has been a solid and steady upward swing, with occasional—and occasionally steep—setbacks. Over time, most investors see a healthy return on their investments.

CHAPTER 5

CONTINUED PROSPERITY

There will always be ups and downs in the stock market. There will be winners and losers. The same people who are winners one day can become losers the next day. The same risk that drives some people away from this kind of money investment can attract others.

Maintaining and Attracting Investors

When a company is successful and makes profits, it can offer some of those profits to its shareholders through quarterly dividends. This makes the idea of buying that company's stock even more attractive to investors. Dividend amounts may be increased or decreased based on the company's performance. A company may also

Opposite: Despite the fact that the economy can seem like a roller coaster, there are still plenty of highs and periods of stability that encourage people to invest.

decide, however, not to give dividends at all. During good economic periods, investors who hold shares in strongly performing companies stand to make a lot of money in dividends. For this reason, stockholders often hold on to their shares in a company instead of constantly selling them at the first sign of a decrease in profits.

Sometimes stock prices may rise too high for new investors to be able to afford them. Remember, people have to purchase shares in order to have them. Other times, a company's stock prices will rise much higher than those of its competitors, making it less attractive to new investors. They won't want to pay a high price for the stock

Even in Monopoly, you can earn dividends. A dividend is an amount that a successful company pays to its shareholders.

when they can buy similar stock in a different company for less. In response, the company's board of directors, a group of people that governs the company, may decide to split the number of shares available for purchase.

This usually means that, for every one share of stock owned, the stockholder will now have two shares of stock. The value of each share will be cut in half. This makes the stock prices half as much as they were before. New investors may now be interested in buying into the company at the new, more affordable rate. They have proof that the company is successful because it just split its stock, a sure sign of strong stock market performance.

Shareholders who already had stock in the company before the split will now have twice the number of shares they once held in the company. However, the overall value of their stock will remain the same. So instead of owning one share at ten dollars, they now own two shares at five dollars each. There are long-term benefits, however, for the existing shareholders with split stocks.

The new, lower price will make the stock more attractive to new investors. When new investors buy into the stock, the prices will be driven up. For example, if the new five-dollar stock goes up another dollar, the original shareholders will then have two shares at six dollars each. So without investing any new money, the original shareholder now has twelve dollars in stocks

All of these numbers might make an individual investor's head spin. For that reason, there are stockbrokers, trained professionals who manage investments for clients.

instead of ten. This rise in the stock's price may not have occurred if not for the influx of new investors. If an investor remains a shareholder for a long time, he or she may experience several splits of a stock, and his or her number of shares will keep doubling.

Attracting and maintaining investors is key to keeping the stock market growing. Equally as important is the health of businesses and the economy. Individual investors, corporations, and the federal government must all work together to keep both the stock market and the economy healthy.

A FEW MORE FACTS

- As important as the stock market it is to the economy, it is critical to remember it's not the best indicator for the health of the economy. In the United States, the federal government pays more attention to the gross domestic product, which represents the value of all goods and services produced in the country in a given period of time. The national unemployment rate is another important indicator.
- Although perhaps not the best indicator about the economy, the stock market does reflect consumer confidence. In other words, it shows how good people are feeling about the economy and how much people are willing to invest in businesses. The stock market also shows how well businesses are doing because people are willing to spend money on their goods and services.
- Investors must be aware of the risks, research their investments, invest only a portion of their savings, and spread their money around to many different companies to minimize the chance of sudden huge losses. If they do these things, investing in the stock market can be a fairly reliable and effective way to increase personal wealth, support American corporations, and keep the economy humming.

GLOSSARY

bear market A period of falling stock prices, which encourages shareholders to sell off their stocks.

bond A loan that an individual gives a company or government, which the borrower promises to pay back with interest in regular installments; this individual can always decide to sell the bond for the full price at any time.

bull market A period of rising stock prices, which encourages shareholders to purchase more stocks.

capitalism An economic system in which trade and industry can be privately owned, rather than government-owned, and designed to make a profit for the owners.

credit history A person's financial record based on that person's track record of paying bills and loans.

dividend The amount of money paid by companies to their shareholders from the company's profits.

economy The resources or wealth of a region or country, as they pertain to the production, sale, and use of goods and services.

Federal Reserve The system of national banks that controls the money supply in the United States.

foreclose To take away a person's property because of failure to keep up with payments.

Great Depression A period of severe economic slowdown that spanned the 1930s.

initial public offering (IPO) The first time a company sells shares of its ownership—stock—to the public.

investor A person who spends money on a company or enterprise and expects to make a profit in return.

prosperity A period of economic success, growth, and wealth.

public company A company that sells shares of its ownership to the public.

recession A natural period of economic slowdown in the business cycle.

securities Certificates of stocks that prove a person's partial ownership of a company.

share A unit of ownership in a company; a share of stock.

stock A unit of ownership in a company.

stock exchange A place in which securities, such as stocks, shares, and bonds, are bought and sold.

subprime mortgage A type of loan to buy a house given to people with low incomes or poor credit scores.

trading The buying and selling of stocks.

Wall Street Named for a defensive wall that used to protect the city, this eight-block stretch in New York City is home to a large portion of the US financial industry; in particular, it is home to the New York Stock Exchange and the NASDAQ. Sometimes, the term "Wall Street" is used as a nickname for the entire US financial sector.

FURTHER INFORMATION

Books

Jones, Keith. *Saving and Investment Information for Teens*. Teen Finance. Detroit: Omnigraphics, 2017.

Kowalski, Kathiann M. *Be Smart About Investing: Planning, Saving, and the Stock Market*. Be Smart About Money and Financial Literacy. New York: Enslow Publishing, 2014.

Mooney, Carla. *Globalization: Why We Care About Faraway Events*. Inquire & Investigate. White River Junction, Vermont: Nomad Press, 2018.

O'Rourke, Ruth, ed. *Heads Up Money*. New York: DK Publishing, 2016.

Peterson, Judy Monroe. *Smart Strategies for Investing Wisely and Successfully*. Financial Security and Life Success for Teens. New York: Rosen Publishing Group, 2015.

Websites

Introduction to Stock Market Investment

https://www.business.illinois.edu/finance_dev

This website provides a complete online course explaining the stock market and investment.

The Mint

http://www.themint.org/teens

This website provides information about money management and investments. Additionally, it has challenges, quizzes, and calculators to help you manage your money and test your financial savvy.

The Stock Market Game

https://www.stockmarketgame.org/expstudent.html

This website will teach you how the stock market works through real-world situations.

Videos

How the 2008 Financial Crisis Crashed the Economy and Changed the World

https://www.youtube.com/watch?v=fXkeh8jiMdk

This video explores how the subprime mortgage crisis affected the stock market and how US bank failures affected the rest of the world.

How the New York Stock Exchange Works

https://www.youtube.com/watch?v=XRJBZIQrQAY

This video provides a brief overview of the daily functions of the New York Stock Exchange.

Organizations

American Association of Individual Investors
625 North Michigan Avenue
Chicago, IL 60611
(800) 428-2244
Website: http://www.aaii.com

The AAII is a nonprofit organization that provides education for individual investors so that they can effectively manage their own investments.

Department of Finance Canada
90 Elgin Street
Ottawa, ON K1A 0G5
Canada
(613) 369-3710
Website: http://www.fin.gc.ca

This governmental department helps to manage the Canadian budget in addition to establishing rules and regulations for Canadian banks and financial institutions.

National Endowment for Financial Education
1331 17th Street, Suite 1200
Denver, CO 80202
(303) 741-6333
Website: http://www.nefe.org

This nonprofit organization provides basic personal finance curriculum geared toward teenagers.

New York Stock Exchange
11 Wall Street
New York, NY 10005
(212) 896-2830
Website: http://www.nyse.com

Established in 1817, the NYSE is the world's largest stock exchange. Its average daily trading value is in the billions of dollars.

Toronto Stock Exchange
130 King Street West
Toronto, ON M5X 1J2
Canada
(416) 947-4700
Website: http://www.tsx.com

Established in 1861, the TSE is one of the world's twenty largest stock exchanges.

US Securities and Exchange Commission
100 F Street NE
Washington, DC 20549
(202) 942-8088
Website: http://www.sec.gov

The SEC oversees the activities of US stock exchanges and stockbrokers. It aims to protect investors and keep the trading of stocks as fair and orderly as possible.

SELECTED BIBLIOGRAPHY

Amadeo, Kimberly. "Auto Industry Bailout: Was the Big 3 Bailout Worth It?" The Balance, November 27, 2018. https://www.thebalance.com/auto-industry-bailout-gm-ford-chrysler-3305670.

———. "Stock Market Crash of 2008: Follow the Timeline to Understand Why It Crashed." The Balance, November 6, 2018. https://www.thebalance.com/stock-market-crash-of-2008-3305535.

Blumenthal, Karen. *Six Days in October: The Stock Market Crash of 1929*. New York: Atheneum Books for Young Readers, 2002.

Calmes, Jackie. "House Passes Stimulus Plan with No GOP Votes." *New York Times*, January 28, 2009. http://www.nytimes.com/2009/01/29/us/politics/29obama.html.

Fraser, Steve. *Wall Street: America's Dream Palace*. New Haven: Yale University Press, 2008.

Kent, Zachary. *The Story of the New York Stock Exchange*. Cornerstones of Freedom. Chicago: Children's Press, 1990.

La Monica, Paul R., and Christine Romans. "Stocks on Track for Worst December Since the Great Depression." CNN Business, December 18, 2018. https://www.cnn.

com/2018/12/18/investing/stocks-worst-december-since-great-depression/index.html.

Little, Ken. "Who's Watching Your Back in Stock Market?: Regulators Are Supposed to Protect You." The Balance, May 30, 2018. https://www.thebalance.com/who-s-watching-your-back-in-stock-market-3141308.

Murray-West, Rosie. "How the Stock Market Works, in Simple Terms." *Telegraph*, September 11, 2015. https://www.telegraph.co.uk/sponsored/finance/investments/climate-environment/11854088/how-stock-market-works.html.

"Our History." ExxonMobile.com. Accessed December 1, 2018. https://corporate.exxonmobil.com/en/company/about-us/history/overview.

Peter, Ian. "History of the Internet: The Dotcom Bubble." NetHistory.com. Accessed December 1, 2018. http://www.nethistory.info/History%20of%20the%20Internet/dotcom.html.

Schoen, John W. "Recession or Depression? Too Early to Tell." NBC News, January 22, 2009. http://www.nbcnews.com/id/28698830/ns/business-personal_finance/#.XA9eB6eZNQI.

Smith, Aaron. "Madoff's Day of Reckoning." CNN.com, June 26, 2009. https://money.cnn.com/2009/06/26/news/economy/madoff_sentence/index.htm.

"What We Do." US Securities and Exchange Commission. Accessed December 1, 2018. http://www.sec.gov/about/whatwedo.shtml.

Whitcrafe, Melissa. *Wall Street.* Cornerstones of Freedom. Chicago: Children's Press, 2003.

Wilson, Andrew B. "Five Myths About the Great Depression." *Wall Street Journal*, November 4, 2008. http://online.wsj.com/article/SB122576077569495545.html.

INDEX

Page numbers in **boldface** refer to images.

ABOUT THE AUTHOR

Chet'la Sebree is a writer, editor, and researcher. She has written and edited several books for Cavendish Square Publishing, including one on the Great Depression. She has degrees in English and creative writing from the University of Richmond and American University, respectively. She is from the Mid-Atlantic region.